Start to Learn
Alphabet

Green Android

Created and produced by:
Green Android Ltd
49 Beaumont Court
Upper Clapton Road
London E5 8BG
United Kingdom
www.greenandroid.co.uk

ISBN 978-1-909244-15-3

Copyright © Green Android Ltd 2013

Acknowledgements

Images © dreamstime.com: drum © Ivashkova.

Images © fotolia.com: aardvark © Eric Isselée; ants © Henrik Larsson, Andrey Pavlov; apple © Dionisvera, margo555, Nattika, Tim UR; Ballerina © Vinicius Tupinamba; balloons © barneyboogles; Beetles (insects) © S.R.Miller, Marianne Mayer, epantha; blocks © Nenov Brothers; Boy (face) © HarmK; car © Maksim Toome, deusexlupus; cushion © karam miri; digger © GOL; emu © Eric Isselée; farm © Elenathewise; feet © Sychugina Elena; fish © Andrey Armyagov, bluehand, crisod, jonnysek, Sergey Skleznev; guitar © Andrey Kuzmin; hats © macau, nuttapongg; ice cream © Viktor; iron © picsfive; jam © Rafa Irusta; kettle © Vlad Ivantcov; kiwi © atoss; leaves © alexfiodorov, Claudio Divizia, Farmer, Fotofermer, volff, Julia Filipenko; lion © Eric Isselée; lollipops © Africa Studio, Elnur; magnet © James Steidl; moon © tdoes; motobikes © adsheyn, Miguel Prado, Navid Hekmat, Photographer; nest © brozova; paper © bennyartist; piano © Yio; piglet © Anatolii; rabbit © xjrshimada; raspberries © volff; recorder © withGod; rocks © maxximmm; sandcastle © elxeneize; stereo (music) © Tengu; stick insect © enskanto; tomato © siro46; toy boat © Isak; umbrella © Artem Merzlenko; underwear © pzAxe; violin © apops; whistle © Ionescu Bogdan; woodpecker © mtruchon; Xylophone © Olha Ukhal, sparkia, trancedrumer, yellowpaul; yogurt © Creatix; yogurt (toppings) © Africa Studio; yoyo © lunamarina; yoyo © Winston Link; zebra © Patryk Kosmider.

Images © Green Android Ltd: drawing, monster mask © Green Android Ltd.

Images © istock.com: ballerina © Gerville.

Images © shutterstock.com: acorns © Alex Staroseltsev; airplane © IM_photo; alligator, chimpanzee, leopard, otter, rabbit © Eric Isselée; ambulance © Glen Jones; anchor © oya979; ankle © Zurijeta; anteaters © Eric Isselee; antelope, ox © Anan Kaewkhammul; apricots © Tim UR, Maks Narodenko, msk.nina; apron, ladder © OZaiachin; arrow © Alvaro Cabrera Jimenez; astronaut © Henrik Lehnerer; astronaut (background) © eddtoro; avocado © gresei, Maks Narodenko; baby, sand © szefei; balls © Richard Peterson, strelov; banana © Tatiana Popova; beads © zimmytws; bike © Gena73; bird © Marina Jay; blackboard © STILLFX; blocks © Nenov Brothers Images; boiled egg © Olga Miltsova; books © gfdunt; box © Mega Pixel; boy (jeans) © Igor Kimov; boy (nose), girl © Samuel Borges Photography; boy (uniform) © michaeljung; boy with umbrella © Sergiy Bykhunenko; boy, queue, family © Andresr; bread © mayakova, Lusoimages; brown recycled paper © makeitdouble; bulldozer © Stanislav Komogorov; bumblebee © vnlit; butterfly © Ambient Ideas; Cactus, milkshake © Joao Virissimo; camel © Roman Gorielov, hainauphoto; cap © turtix; carrot © victoriaKh, showice; castle © Matt Gibson; cat © Scorpp; caterpillar © Jung Hsuan; chameleon © fivespots; clock © inxti, Herminia Lucia Lopes Serra de Casais, Ma-Fot; coins (money) © Asaf Eliason; comb © Chatchai Somwat; cowboy © Gregory Johnston; cows © xtrekx; cream armchair © Mostphotos; crocodile © Andrew Burgess, John Kasawa; cupcake © Ruth Black; cups © hxdbzxy; deer © Vishnevskiy Vasily; desert © apdesign; dice © Dani Simmonds; dinosaurs © Lucie Lang; doctor © Daniel Gale; dolls © bat-2; dolphin © Richard Fitzer; domino, vest © pzAxe; doughnut © Bryan Solomon; matin; dragonfly © butterfly hunter; drum © KariDesign; drummer (quartet) © Phaitoon Sutunyawatchai; duck, pigeon © panbazil; eagle © KarSol; ear, fairy, pirate © Vinicius Tupinamba; earmuff © Petr Malyshev; earrings © photosync; Earth, quartz ©MarcelClemens; earthworm © schankz; easel © ILYA AKINSHIN; egg © Maks Narodenko, rangizzz; elbow © Linda Parton; elephant © Aaron Amat, gualtiero boffi; emerald © Imfoto; envelopes © Daniela Pelazza, Nattika; eraser © Francesco Ocello, oksana2010; eyes © Zurijeta; face cloth © sagir; fan © F. JIMENEZ MECA's ; feather © jps; feet © Smit; field © Sunny Forest; finger © Tomnamon; fire engine © l i g h t p o e t; fireman © KellyBoreson; flag © AJancso; flowers © Sergio33; fly © irin-k; fork, ice cubes, wok, wool © Africa Studio; fox © Pim Leijen; frog © Dirk Ercken; girl (tongue) © iko; girl (uniform) © Michal Kowalski; girl with colourful dress © Nolte Lourens; graph paper © optimarc; grasshopper (insects) © kotoru; guitar player (quartet) © SLP_London; ice cream © Dan Kosmayer, gresei, M. Unal Ozmen, Boule; ice skates © Paleka; icebergs © Volodymyr Goinyk; igloo © Rita Januskeviciute; iguana, monkey © Volodymyr Burdiak; impala © Karel Gallas; ink © Blinka; island © Johan_R; jack-in-the-box © Lusoimages; jackest © kakas; jaguar, volcano © Ammit Jack; jars © Alex Staroseltsev, Africa Studio, rineca; jeep © Jaroslaw Grudzinski; jellybeans © Diana Taliun, mayakova; jet © i4lcocl2; jetski © wizdata; jewels © Byjeng; jungle © Zoom Team; Kangaroo © veroxdale; kennel © tkemot; ketchup © Evgeny Karandaev; keyboard © Iakov Filimonov; keyboard player (quartet) © Ewa Studio; keys © donatas1205; king, queen © Bonita R. Cheshier; Kingfisher © Super Prin; kite © luchunyu; kitten © Ermolaev Alexander; knees, legs © Jiri Hera; knight © Marcin-linfernum; knot © lenetstan; koala © worldswildlifewonders; ladybird © Sebastian Knight; lamb © Richard Waters; lettuce © greatstockimages; lightbulb © imstock; lighthouse © brackish_nz; lime, lemon © Ian 2010; limousine © Christopher Halloran; lips © varandah; log © Sebastian Knight; mango, melon © Viktar Malyshchyts; milk © Serhiy Kobyakov; mirror © lasha; mittens © VikaRayu; mop © Sopotnicki; motobike © MiloVad; mountains © Vladimir Sklyarov; mouse © ivosar; mushrooms © saras66; neck © aporokh at gmail dot com; necklace © Dmitry Kolmakov; needle © Sar_38; net © terekhov igor; newspaper © RTimages; newt © JGade; night © Celso Diniz; noodles © Viktor1; notebooks © kak2s; notes © Elnur; nurse © glenda; nuts © Artem Samokhvalov, Mamuka Gotsiridze, vblinov, Dionisvera; ocean © chbaum; octopus © Shane Gross; oil can © VR Photos; oil leak © Jamen Percy; olives © Drozdowski; onion © KIM NGUYEN; oranges © JIANG HONGYAN; orangutan © Nagel Photography; ostrich © Dhoxax; overalls © RimDream; owl © Joe West; Padlock © BorisShevchuk; Paintbrush © Nuttapong; pajamas, underwear © Olga Popova; Paper © R-studio; paper clip © Madlen; parrot © pr2is; pencil © Quang Ho, DenisNata; penguin © Dmytro Pylypenko; Peppers © Shahsuvar Asadov; pineapple © Nattika; Pizza © TRL; plates © Deymos Photo; policegirl © Michelle D. Milliman; potato © AlenKadr, Nattika; puffin © francesco de marco; pumpkin © topseller; pyjamas © Khvost; quad bike © Art Konovalov; quail © Sergey Goruppa; quiche © Iorga Studio; quilt © Aerostato; raccoon © Ultrashock; rake © Artur Ish; recorder player (quartet) © Rachwalski Andrzej; red airchair © Ad Oculos; rhinoceros © Andy Dean Photography; ribbon © Shebeko; rice © Freer; river © Yuriy Kulik; road © tarasov; robot © studio BM; rope © Ratthaphong Ekariyasap; rose © max777; scarf © Karkas; scissors © Vladvm; shoes © Larisa Lofitskaya; Stag Beetle © Melinda fawver; tissue paper © Pefkos; tractor © alexmisu; truck © auremar; ukuleles © Artter, Wuttichok Painichiwarapun; umbrellas © aldegonde, Nathalie Photography, PHB.cz (Richard Semik); unicorn © Natelle; vacuum cleaner © WM_idea; vase © Gavran333; vehicles © Maryna Pleshkun, Karramba Production; venus fly trap © Cathy Keifer; Vinegar © Danny Smythe; violin © Sergey_Bogomyako; wall © loreanto; wallet © Ian 2010; watch © Polryaz; waterfall © grafvision; watermelon © AN NGUYEN; wheel © ia_64, Realchemyst, steamroller_blues; whistle © LU HUANFENG; windmills © KIM NGUYEN; windows © chrupka; wolf © Maxim Kulko; wood © Alekss; Xylophone © bright; yachts © Jules_Kitano; yak © eAlisa; Yam © zcw; yoke © isak55; yoyo © design56, HomeStudio, joppo, Renewer, gdvcom, Katrina Leigh; zebra head © Therina Groenewald; zip © NorGal; zoo sign © Becky Stares.

All rights reserved. No part of this publication may be reproduced, stored in a retrieval system, or transmitted in any form or by any means, electronic, mechanical, photocopying, recording or otherwise without the prior written permission of the publisher.

Please note that every effort has been made to check the accuracy of the information contained in this book, and to credit the copyright holders correctly. Green Android Ltd apologize for any unintentional errors or omissions, and would be happy to include revisions to content and/or acknowledgements in subsequent editions of this book.

Printed and bound in China, October 2013

Note to parents and carers

Start to Learn Alphabet is an exciting way to teach your child the letters and sounds they need in order to read, spell and write. With over 500 words and colourful pictures there are lots of things to talk about together.

Help your child develop literacy skills by pointing to the clear labels as you name each picture and letter.

Designed as a fun learning experience, Start to Learn Alphabet will entertain, as well as educate, young children for many hours.

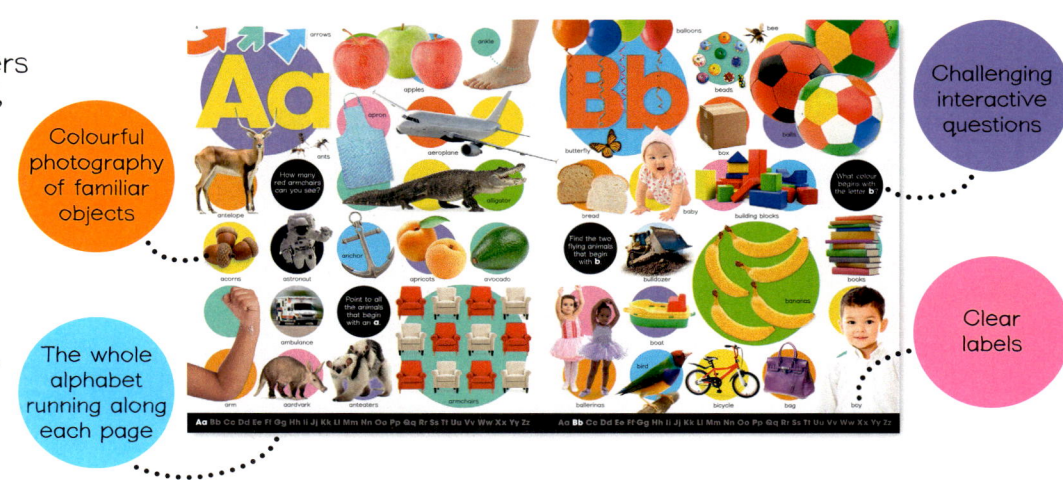

- Colourful photography of familiar objects
- The whole alphabet running along each page
- Challenging interactive questions
- Clear labels

Contents

- **4** All the letters
- **6** Aa
- **7** Bb
- **8** Cc
- **9** Dd
- **10** Ee
- **11** Ff
- **12** Gg
- **13** Hh
- **14** Ii
- **15** Jj
- **16** Kk
- **17** Ll
- **18** Mm
- **19** Nn
- **20** Oo
- **21** Pp
- **22** Qq
- **23** Rr
- **24** Ss
- **25** Tt
- **26** Uu
- **27** Vv
- **28** Ww
- **29** Xx
- **30** Yy
- **31** Zz
- **32** Odd one out

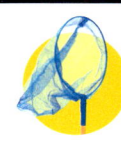

A B C D E F G H I J K L M

All the letters

Aa — a is for apple

Bb — b is for boy

Cc — c is for cat

Hh — h is for hat

Ii — i is for ice cream

Jj — j is for jellybeans

Kk — k is for king

Pp — p is for penguin

Qq — q is for queen

Rr — r is for robot

Ss — s is for sandcastle

Xx — x is for xylophone

Yy — y is for yogurt

Zz — z is for zebra

How many letters are there in the alphabet?

a b c d e f g h i j k l m

N O P Q R S T U V W X Y Z

Dd d is for drum

Ee e is for egg

Ff f is for fork

Gg g is for girl

Ll l is for leaf

Mm m is for mask

Nn n is for nuts

Oo o is for orange

Tt t is for tomato

Uu u is for umbrella

Vv v is for violin

Ww w is for whistle

Point to the letter that your name begins with.

What other animals begin with the letter c?

What keeps the rain off and begins with u?

n o p q r s t u v w x y z

Aa

arrows

apples

ankle

antelope

ants

apron

aeroplane

alligator

How many red armchairs can you see?

acorns

astronaut

anchor

apricots

avocado

arm

ambulance

Point to all the animals that begin with an **a**.

aardvark

anteaters

armchairs

Aa Bb Cc Dd Ee Ff Gg Hh Ii Jj Kk Ll Mm Nn Oo Pp Qq Rr Ss Tt Uu Vv Ww Xx Yy Zz

Bb

balloons

bee

beads

butterfly

box

balls

bread

baby

building blocks

What colour begins with the letter **b**?

Find the three flying animals that begin with **b**.

bulldozer

bananas

books

boat

ballerinas

bird

bicycle

bag

boy

Aa **Bb** Cc Dd Ee Ff Gg Hh Ii Jj Kk Ll Mm Nn Oo Pp Qq Rr Ss Tt Uu Vv Ww Xx Yy Zz

circle

cars

Cc

chimpanzee

castle

cushion

chalk

crocodile

chameleon

Which shape begins with the letter c?

comb

cows

candle

cakes

cowboy

carrots

cheese

How many clocks can you find?

camel

cactus

cat

clocks

caterpillar

cups

cap

Aa Bb **Cc** Dd Ee Ff Gg Hh Ii Jj Kk Ll Mm Nn Oo Pp Qq Rr Ss Tt Uu Vv Ww Xx Yy Zz

down

Dd

dinosaurs

doors

Where are the two noisy vehicles?

diamond

deer

dice

doughnuts

dog   duck   desert

dump truck

drums

dress

drawing

dominoes   dolphin

What tasty treats begin with **d**?

doctor   doll

digger

Aa Bb Cc **Dd** Ee Ff Gg Hh Ii Jj Kk Ll Mm Nn Oo Pp Qq Rr Ss Tt Uu Vv Ww Xx Yy Zz

Ee

exclamation marks

Earth

earthworm

erasers

easel

ear

Which body parts begin with the letter **e**?

envelopes

emu

emerald

elephants

earrings

eyelashes

eye

eggs

eagle

earmuffs

How many envelopes are there?

elbow

Aa Bb Cc Dd **Ee** Ff Gg Hh Ii Jj Kk Ll Mm Nn Oo Pp Qq Rr Ss Tt Uu Vv Ww Xx Yy Zz

fish

Ff

Point to the pink bird beginning with **f**?

fan

feet

feather

forks

farm

finger

flag

fly

flowers

fire engine

field

family

frog

How many forks can you see?

flamingo

face cloth

face

fox

fairy

fire fighter

Aa Bb Cc Dd Ee **Ff** Gg Hh Ii Jj Kk Ll Mm Nn Oo Pp Qq Rr Ss Tt Uu Vv Ww Xx Yy Zz

Gg

guitars

glass

gorilla

gloves

Can you see some fruits that begin with **g**?

gift bags

globe

grapefruit

goat

glue

goose

gate

Point to a tall animal beginning with **g**.

grapes

guinea pig

giraffe

grass

glasses

goggles

girl

goldfish

Aa Bb Cc Dd Ee Ff **Gg** Hh Ii Jj Kk Ll Mm Nn Oo Pp Qq Rr Ss Tt Uu Vv Ww Xx Yy Zz

Hh

hot-air balloons

honey

hammers

heel

hats

hens

hair

What prickly animal begins with **h**?

harmonica

hamburger

horse

heart

hexagon

hairclips

Which shapes begin with the letter **h**?

hedgehog

helicopter

hand

hanger

hamster

hippopotamus

house

Aa Bb Cc Dd Ee Ff Gg **Hh** Ii Jj Kk Ll Mm Nn Oo Pp Qq Rr Ss Tt Uu Vv Ww Xx Yy Zz

Ii

insects

How many ice creams can you see?

iguana

impala

island

ice cubes

igloos

iron

Which scaly animal begins with **i**?

ice skates

ink

ice creams

icebergs

Aa Bb Cc Dd Ee Ff Gg Hh **Ii** Jj Kk Ll Mm Nn Oo Pp Qq Rr Ss Tt Uu Vv Ww Xx Yy Zz

Jj

jewels
jet
juice
jet ski
jungle
jam
What type of drink begins with **j**?
jeep
jellyfish
What flies in the air and begins with **j**?
jigsaw puzzle
jars
jelly beans
jack-in-the-box
jaguar
jeans
jackets

Aa Bb Cc Dd Ee Ff Gg Hh Ii **Jj** Kk Ll Mm Nn Oo Pp Qq Rr Ss Tt Uu Vv Ww Xx Yy Zz

Kk

keys

knees

kennel

What gets very hot and begins with **k**?

kangaroo

kite

king

kiwi fruit

knot

ketchup

knives

kitten

keyboard

koala

Which animal hops and begins with **k**?

knight

kettle

kingfisher

Aa Bb Cc Dd Ee Ff Gg Hh Ii Jj **Kk** Ll Mm Nn Oo Pp Qq Rr Ss Tt Uu Vv Ww Xx Yy Zz lollipops

Ll

lip

ladybird

log

letters

legs

lion

leopard

lettuce

lamp

lemon

Which spotty insect begins with l?

lightbulb

limousine

lime

leaves

ladder

Point to a vegetable that begins with l?

lighthouse

lamb

Aa Bb Cc Dd Ee Ff Gg Hh Ii Jj Kk **Ll** Mm Nn Oo Pp Qq Rr Ss Tt Uu Vv Ww Xx Yy Zz

Mm

Moon

mountain

mirror

Point to two drinks that begin with **m**.

mittens

music

mugs

mushrooms

mouth

milk

masks

mouse

What can you wear that begins with **m**?

melon

mango

magnet

money

monkey

milkshake

motorbikes

mop

Aa Bb Cc Dd Ee Ff Gg Hh Ii Jj Kk Ll **Mm** Nn Oo Pp Qq Rr Ss Tt Uu Vv Ww Xx Yy Zz

Nn

nuts

noodles

numbers

needle

How many napkins can you find?

nest

notebook

notes

newt

neck

nose

necklace

night

nets

napkins

nurse

nails

newspaper

What is used for sewing and begins with **n**?

Aa Bb Cc Dd Ee Ff Gg Hh Ii Jj Kk Ll Mm **Nn** Oo Pp Qq Rr Ss Tt Uu Vv Ww Xx Yy Zz

20

1 one

owl

oranges

onion

ocelot

oryx

ostrich

octopus

olives

What is a type of fruit that begin with **o**?

ox

otter

octagon

oval

orca

oil

ocean

What small number begins with **o**?

overalls

orang-utan

Aa Bb Cc Dd Ee Ff Gg Hh Ii Jj Kk Ll Mm Nn **Oo** Pp Qq Rr Ss Tt Uu Vv Ww Xx Yy Zz

Pp

puffin

pentagon

pizza

What pink animal begins with **p**?

polar bear

pens

plates

pineapple

pirate

pepper

pumpkin

potatoes

pyjamas

paper

pad

piano

padlock

parrot

paperclips

pencils

paintbrush

pigeon

paints

pig

pretzels

police officer

What is a shape that begins with **p**?

penguins

Aa Bb Cc Dd Ee Ff Gg Hh Ii Jj Kk Ll Mm Nn Oo **Pp** Qq Rr Ss Tt Uu Vv Ww Xx Yy Zz

Qq

question marks

Point to the animal that begins with q.

queue

quartz

quiche

quad bike

quarters

queen

quail

quilt

What can you eat that begins with q?

quartet

Aa Bb Cc Dd Ee Ff Gg Hh Ii Jj Kk Ll Mm Nn Oo Pp **Qq** Rr Ss Tt Uu Vv Ww Xx Yy Zz

Rr

rulers

rectangle

racing car

raspberries

rice

rings

What can you wear that begins with r?

raccoon

What is made of water and begins with r?

rose

ribbon

rubber ducks

rope

rake

rocket

recorder

robots

rabbit

road

rocks

river

rhinoceros

Aa Bb Cc Dd Ee Ff Gg Hh Ii Jj Kk Ll Mm Nn Oo Pp Qq **Rr** Ss Tt Uu Vv Ww Xx Yy Zz

Ss

stars

soap

socks

shampoo

seahorses

starfish

slippers

shoes

shorts

sandals

snake

scarf

strawberries

sunflowers

Which slithering animal begins with **s**?

salt

snail

scissors

What has lots of legs and begins with **s**?

spider

sea

sandcastle

shell

sandwich

salad

spade

sand

Aa Bb Cc Dd Ee Ff Gg Hh Ii Jj Kk Ll Mm Nn Oo Pp Qq Rr **Ss** Tt Uu Vv Ww Xx Yy Zz

Tt

trumpets

10 ten

turtle

television

teddy bear

twins

telephone

toothpaste

toothbrush

tools

towels

Which animal is on the television?

table

tortoise

train

t-shirt

toast

tricycle

triangle

tiger

tambourine

toucan

tomatoes

toes

thumb

tongue

tractor

tree

What can you cuddle that begins with t?

Aa Bb Cc Dd Ee Ff Gg Hh Ii Jj Kk Ll Mm Nn Oo Pp Qq Rr Ss **Tt** Uu Vv Ww Xx Yy Zz

Uu

underwear

unicorn

How many umbrellas can you see?

uniform

up

ukuleles

Point to the cycle that begins with **u**.

unicycle

umbrellas

Aa Bb Cc Dd Ee Ff Gg Hh Ii Jj Kk Ll Mm Nn Oo Pp Qq Rr Ss Tt **Uu** Vv Ww Xx Yy Zz

Vv

vegetables

volcano

vacuum cleaner

venus fly trap

violin

vinegar

vest

What can you wear that begins with **v**?

vulture

Which group of food begins with **v**?

vehicles

vase

Aa Bb Cc Dd Ee Ff Gg Hh Ii Jj Kk Ll Mm Nn Oo Pp Qq Rr Ss Tt Uu **Vv** Ww Xx Yy Zz

Ww

wheels
wok
whale
wand
watch
waterfall
woodpecker
window
witch
wool
What can you drink that begins with **w**?
wall
wolf
What can you cook with that begins with **w**?
whistle
water
wood
wallet
watermelon
windmill
walrus

Aa Bb Cc Dd Ee Ff Gg Hh Ii Jj Kk Ll Mm Nn Oo Pp Qq Rr Ss Tt Uu Vv **Ww** Xx Yy Zz

Xx

X-rays

xylophones

What musical instrument begins with **x**?

What type of picture shows your bones?

Aa Bb Cc Dd Ee Ff Gg Hh Ii Jj Kk Ll Mm Nn Oo Pp Qq Rr Ss Tt Uu Vv Ww **Xx** Yy Zz

Yy

yo-yos

How many yo-yos can you see?

yachts

yak

yolk

yogurts

yams

What colour begins with the letter **y**?

Aa Bb Cc Dd Ee Ff Gg Hh Ii Jj Kk Ll Mm Nn Oo Pp Qq Rr Ss Tt Uu Vv Ww Xx **Yy** Zz

Zoo

Zz

0 zero

Which stripy animals begin with **z**?

zig zags

zebras

zip

Which type of line begins with **z**?

Aa Bb Cc Dd Ee Ff Gg Hh Ii Jj Kk Ll Mm Nn Oo Pp Qq Rr Ss Tt Uu Vv Ww Xx Yy **Zz**

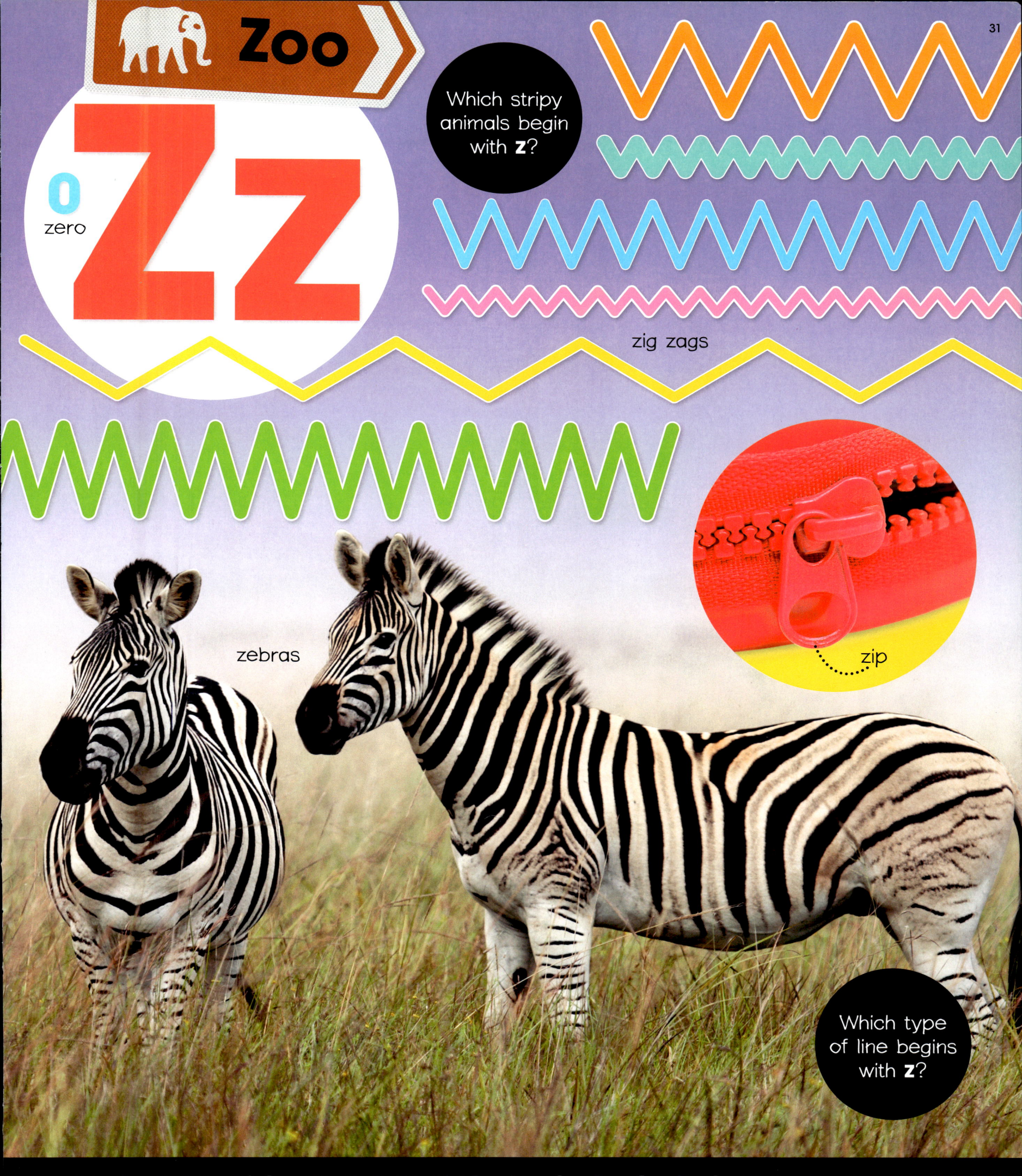

Odd one out

Each group of items should start with the same letter.
Can you find the odd one out in each group?

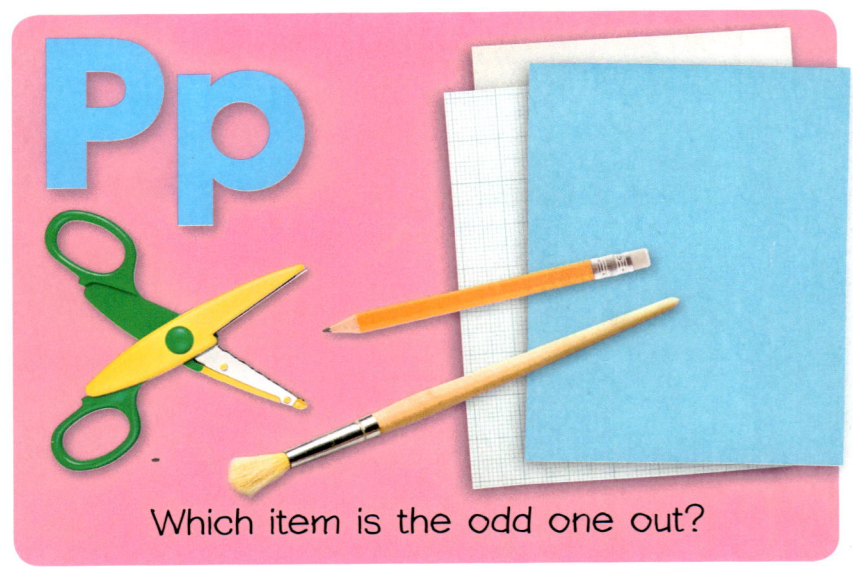

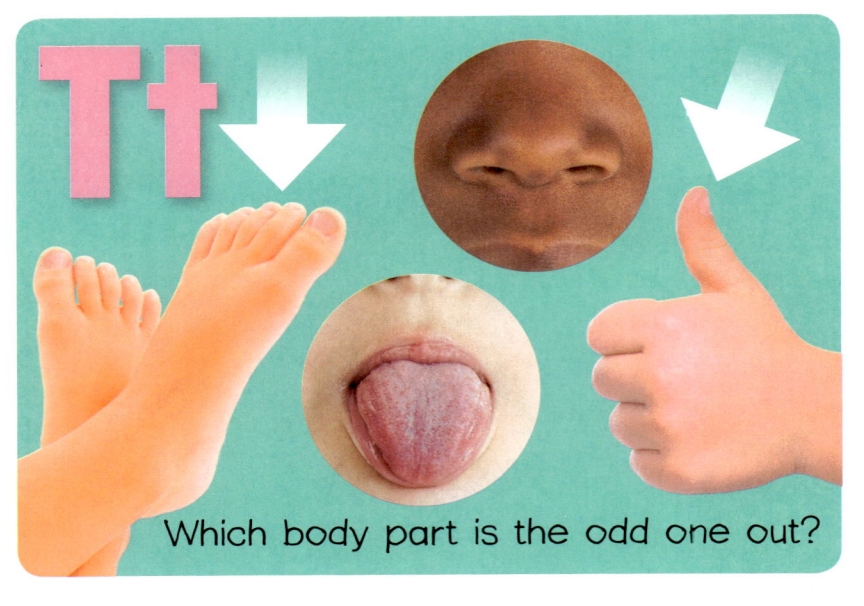

Ss — Which is the odd one out in this group?

Bb — Which toy is the odd one out?

Pp — Which item is the odd one out?

Aa — Which fruit is the odd one out?

Cc — Which animal is the odd one out?

Tt — Which body part is the odd one out?

Aa Bb Cc Dd Ee Ff Gg Hh Ii Jj Kk Ll Mm Nn Oo Pp Qq Rr Ss Tt Uu Vv Ww Xx Yy Zz